I0469112

March 2012

DOE LOAN GUARANTEES

Further Actions Are Needed to Improve Tracking and Review of Applications

GAO

Accountability ★ Integrity ★ Reliability

GAO
Accountability * Integrity * Reliability

Highlights

Highlights of GAO-12-157, a report to congressional committees

DOE LOAN GUARANTEES

Further Actions Are Needed to Improve Tracking and Review of Applications

Why GAO Did This Study

The Department of Energy's (DOE) Loan Guarantee Program (LGP) was created by section 1703 of the Energy Policy Act of 2005 to guarantee loans for innovative energy projects. Currently, DOE is authorized to make up to $34 billion in section 1703 loan guarantees. In February 2009, the American Recovery and Reinvestment Act added section 1705, making certain commercial technologies that could start construction by September 30, 2011, eligible for loan guarantees. It provided $6 billion in appropriations that were later reduced by transfer and rescission to $2.5 billion. The funds could cover DOE's costs for an estimated $18 billion in additional loan guarantees. GAO has an ongoing mandate to review the program's implementation. Because of concerns raised in prior work, GAO assessed (1) the status of the applications to the LGP and (2) for loans that the LGP has committed to, or made, the extent to which the program has adhered to its process for reviewing applications. GAO analyzed relevant legislation, regulations, and guidance; prior audits; and LGP data, documents, and applications. GAO also interviewed DOE officials and private lenders with experience in energy project lending.

What GAO Recommends

GAO recommends that the Secretary of Energy establish a timetable for, and fully implement, a consolidated system to provide information on LGP applications and reviews and regularly update program policies and procedures. DOE disagreed with the first of GAO's three recommendations; GAO continues to believe that a consolidated system would enhance program management.

View GAO-12-157. For more information, contact Frank Rusco at (202) 512-3841 or ruscof@gao.gov.

What GAO Found

The Department of Energy (DOE) has made $15 billion in loan guarantees and conditionally committed to an additional $15 billion, but the program does not have the consolidated data on application status needed to facilitate efficient management and program oversight. For the 460 applications to the Loan Guarantee Program (LGP), DOE has made loan guarantees for 7 percent and committed to an additional 2 percent. The time the LGP took to review loan applications decreased over the course of the program, according to GAO's analysis of LGP data. However, when GAO requested data from the LGP on the status of these applications, the LGP did not have consolidated data readily available and had to assemble these data over several months from various sources. Without consolidated data on applicants, LGP managers do not have readily accessible information that would facilitate more efficient program management, and LGP staff may not be able to identify weaknesses, if any, in the program's application review process and approval procedures. Furthermore, because it took months to assemble the data required for GAO's review, it is also clear that the data were not readily available to conduct timely oversight of the program. LGP officials have acknowledged the need for a consolidated system and said that the program has begun developing a comprehensive business management system that could also be used to track the status of LGP applications. However, the LGP has not committed to a timetable to fully implement this system.

The LGP adhered to most of its established process for reviewing applications, but its actual process differed from its established process at least once on 11 of the 13 applications GAO reviewed. Private lenders who finance energy projects that GAO interviewed found that the LGP's established review process was generally as stringent as or more stringent than their own. However, GAO found that the reviews that the LGP conducted sometimes differed from its established process in that, for example, actual reviews skipped applicable review steps. In other cases, GAO could not determine whether the LGP had performed some established review steps because of poor documentation. Omitting or poorly documenting reviews reduces the LGP's assurance that it has treated applicants consistently and equitably and, in some cases, may affect the LGP's ability to fully assess and mitigate project risks. Furthermore, the absence of adequate documentation may make it difficult for DOE to defend its decisions on loan guarantees as sound and fair if it is questioned about the justification for and equity of those decisions. One cause of the differences between established and actual processes was that, according to LGP staff, they were following procedures that had been revised but were not yet updated in the credit policies and procedures manual, which governs much of the LGP's established review process. In particular, the version of the manual in use at the time of GAO's review was dated March 5, 2009, even though the manual states it was meant to be updated at least annually, and more frequently as needed. The updated manual dated October 6, 2011, addresses many of the differences GAO identified. Officials also demonstrated that LGP had taken steps to address the documentation issues by beginning to implement its new document management system. However, by the close of GAO's review, LGP could not provide sufficient documentation to resolve the issues identified in the review.

_____ **United States Government Accountability Office**

Contents

Figures

Abbreviations

CRB	Credit Review Board
DOE	Department of Energy
EERE	Energy Efficiency, Renewable Energy
FIPP	Financial Institution Partnership Program
LGP	Loan Guarantee Program
LPO	Loan Programs Office
OMB	Office of Management and Budget

United States Government Accountability Office
Washington, DC 20548

March 12, 2012

The Honorable Dianne Feinstein
Chair
The Honorable Lamar Alexander
Ranking Member
Subcommittee on Energy and Water Development
Committee on Appropriations
United States Senate

The Honorable Rodney P. Frelinghuysen
Chairman
The Honorable Peter J. Visclosky
Ranking Member
Subcommittee on Energy and Water Development,
    and Related Agencies
Committee on Appropriations
House of Representatives

The Department of Energy's (DOE) loan guarantee program (LGP) is currently authorized to issue loan guarantees worth up to $34 billion for certain types of energy projects that need affordable financing.[1] Federal loan guarantee programs such as the LGP can help companies obtain such financing because the federal government agrees to reimburse the lender for the guaranteed amount if a borrower defaults. As directed by section 1703 of the Energy Policy Act of 2005, the LGP originally focused on projects that use new or significantly improved energy technologies and avoid, reduce, or sequester emissions of air pollutants or man-made greenhouse gases. In February 2009, Congress expanded the scope of the LGP in the American Recovery and Reinvestment Act (Recovery Act), by adding section 1705 to the Energy Policy Act, which provided funding and extended the program to include projects that use commercial energy technology that employs renewable energy systems, electric power transmission systems, or leading-edge biofuels that meet certain criteria. The LGP has issued nine calls for applications—known as solicitations— each of which covers particular types of energy technology.

---

[1]The amount of authority does not include approximately $20 billion that expired when authority for a portion of the program expired on September 30, 2011.

GAO-12-157 DOE Loan Guarantees

According to DOE officials, the LGP is important to both develop new energy technologies for commercial use and make some commercial projects possible, thereby creating jobs and new energy supplies. However, loan guarantee programs can also expose the government to substantial financial risks. For example, a borrower could default on a federally guaranteed loan, leaving taxpayers to pay for the loss. In the past, we also found problems with federal loan guarantee programs that occurred in part because agencies did not exercise sufficient due diligence. Due diligence is the review process by which a lender identifies and mitigates potential problems or risks with a project before the lender makes a loan or loan guarantee. Recently, the filing of bankruptcy petitions by two recipients of DOE loan guarantees have raised concerns that DOE may not be sufficiently identifying and mitigating the risk of a loan default.

GAO has an ongoing mandate under the 2007 Revised Continuing Appropriations Resolution to review DOE's execution of the LGP and to report its findings to the House and Senate Committees on Appropriations. This is the sixth time we have reported on this program.[2] We have raised concerns in our prior work about the limitations of the portion of the program conducted under section 1703 in attracting financially viable projects representing the full range of targeted technologies.[3] In addition, we previously reported, among other things, that the LGP treated applicants inconsistently and recommended that DOE treat applicants consistently or clearly establish the conditions that would warrant disparate treatment.[4] Because of questions regarding inconsistent treatment of applicants and DOE's review process that we raised in the 2010 report, our objectives for this report were to determine (1) the status of the applications to the LGP's nine solicitations and (2) the extent to which the LGP has adhered to its process for reviewing applications for loans that the LGP has committed to or closed.

---

[2]See our list of related products on the LGP at the end of this report.

[3]GAO, *Department of Energy: New Loan Guarantee Program Should Complete Activities Necessary for Effective and Accountable Program Management,* GAO-08-750 (Washington, D.C.: July 7, 2008).

[4]GAO-08-750; GAO, *Department of Energy: Further Actions Are Needed to Improve DOE's Ability to Evaluate and Implement the Loan Guarantee Program,* GAO-10-627 (Washington, D.C.: July 12, 2010).

To determine the status of applications to the LGP's nine solicitations, we reviewed DOE and LGP documents on the establishment and operation of the program and analyzed the LGP's available data on the applications received and their current status. Because the LGP did not maintain consolidated information on application status, it had to assemble data from various sources for all of the applications as of September 30, 2011. To assist in this effort, we tailored a data request to collect data on the status of all 460 applications to the program in consultation with agency officials. These data were to provide a current snapshot of the program by solicitation and allow analysis of various characteristics. LGP staff familiar with each solicitation completed the spreadsheets, and these spreadsheets were reviewed by managers before they were forwarded to GAO. We assessed the reliability of the data the LGP provided by reviewing it, comparing it to other sources and following up with the agency to clarify questions and inconsistencies, and obtain missing data. Once the data were all collected, we found them to be sufficiently reliable for our purposes. This process enabled us to develop up-to-date programwide information on the status of applications. The LGP staff updated its March 2011 applicant status data as of July 29, 2011, and we obtained additional data on the conditional commitments and closings made by the September 30, 2011, expiration of the section 1705 authority for loan guarantees with a credit subsidy. In cases where multiple applications were submitted for a single project, we considered each to be a single application for purposes of this report. In addition, we met with the LGP's management and staff from each of the divisions involved with the review process. To determine the extent to which the LGP has adhered to its process for reviewing applications for loans that it has committed to or closed, we identified the key steps in the review process by analyzing the laws, regulations, policies, guidance, and solicitations for the program. We verified these key steps in interviews with LGP officials. We identified the 13 applications that had received conditional commitments or had closed by December 31, 2010.[5] We then requested documentation from the LGP of the key review steps it conducted for selected applications. We initially requested this documentation for a

---

[5]Three additional applications had either reached conditional commitment or closed during this period. We excluded these applications from our review because the LGP's review process for these applications was substantially different. A conditional commitment is a commitment by DOE to issue a loan guarantee if the applicant satisfies specific requirements. The Secretary of Energy has the discretion to cancel a conditional commitment at any time for any reason prior to the issuance of a loan guarantee.

nonprobability sample of 6 applications representing a range of solicitations and project types.[6] We also collected more limited information on the 7 remaining applications to which DOE had conditionally committed to issue a loan guarantee by the end of calendar year 2010. For these 7, we reviewed certain key steps for which we found differences from the LGP's established process during our review of the initial 6 applications. We did not evaluate the quality of the LGP's analyses supporting the completion of these steps. The applications we reviewed were processed by the LGP under the policies and procedures that were in place through September 30, 2011.[7] We also interviewed seven private lenders with experience financing energy sector projects to gain insights on the comparability of the LGP and private sector review processes. A more detailed discussion of our objectives, scope, and methodology is presented in appendix I.

We conducted this performance audit from September 2010 to February 2012 in accordance with generally accepted government auditing standards. Those standards require that we plan and perform the audit to obtain sufficient, appropriate evidence to provide a reasonable basis for our findings and conclusions based on our audit objectives. We believe that the evidence obtained provides a reasonable basis for our findings and conclusions based on our audit objectives.

Background

DOE's LGP was designed to address the fundamental impediment for investors that stems from the high risks of clean energy projects, including technology risk—the risk that the new technology will not perform as expected—and execution risk—the risk that the borrower will not perform as expected. Companies can face obstacles in securing enough affordable financing to survive the "valley of death" between developing innovative technologies and commercializing them. Because the risks that lenders must assume to support new technologies can put private financing out of reach, companies may not be able to commercialize innovative technologies without the federal government's

---

[6]Because this was a nonprobability sample, we cannot generalize what we found to all applications, but we chose these applications to include a variety of project types and for different solicitations.

[7]Department of Energy, *Title XVII Of The Energy Policy Act Of 2005 Loan Guarantee Program, Credit Policies and Procedures* (Washington, D.C., Mar. 5, 2009).

financial support. According to the DOE loan program's Executive Director, DOE loan guarantees lower the cost of capital for projects using innovative energy technologies, making them more competitive with conventional technologies and thus more attractive to lenders and equity investors. Moreover, according to the DOE loan programs Executive Director, the program takes advantage of DOE's expertise in analyzing the technical aspects of proposed projects, which can be difficult for private sector lenders without that expertise.

Until February 2009, the LGP was working exclusively under section 1703 of the Energy Policy Act of 2005, which authorized loan guarantees for new or innovative energy technologies that had not yet been commercialized. Congress had authorized DOE to guarantee approximately $34 billion in section 1703 loans by fiscal year 2009, after accounting for rescissions, but it did not appropriate funds to pay the "credit subsidy costs" of these guarantees. For section 1703 loan guarantees, each applicant was to pay the credit subsidy cost of its own project. These costs are defined as the estimated long-term cost, in net present value terms, over the entire period the loans are outstanding to cover interest subsidies, defaults, and delinquencies (not including administrative costs). Under the Federal Credit Reform Act of 1990, the credit subsidy cost for any guaranteed loan must be provided prior to a loan guarantee commitment.

In past reports, we found several issues with the LGP's implementation of section 1703. For example, in our July 2008 report, we stated that risks inherent to the program make it difficult for DOE to estimate credit subsidy costs it charges to borrowers.[8] If DOE underestimates these costs, taxpayers will ultimately bear the costs of defaults or other shortfalls not covered by the borrowers' payments into a cost-subsidy pool that is to cover section 1703's program-wide costs of default. In addition, we reported that, to the extent that certain types of projects or technologies are more likely than others to have fees that are too high to remain economically viable, the projects that do accept guarantees may be more heavily weighted toward lower-risk technologies and may not represent the full range of technologies targeted by the section 1703 program.

---

[8]GAO-08-750.

In February 2009, the Recovery Act amended the Energy Policy Act of 2005, authorizing the LGP to guarantee loans under section 1705. This section also provided $2.5 billion to pay applicants' credit subsidy costs.[9] This credit subsidy funding was available only to projects that began construction by September 30, 2011, among other requirements.[10] DOE estimated that the funding would be sufficient to provide about $18 billion in guarantees under section 1705. Section 1705 authorized guarantees for commercial energy projects that employ renewable energy systems, electric power transmission systems, or leading-edge biofuels that meet certain criteria. Some of these are the same types of projects eligible under section 1703, which authorizes guarantees only for projects that use new or significantly improved technologies.[11] Consequently, many projects that had applied under section 1703 became eligible to have their credit subsidy costs paid under section 1705.

---

[9]Pub. L. No. 111-5, Div. A, Title IV (Feb. 17, 2009). Congress originally appropriated nearly $6 billion to pay the credit subsidy costs of projects supported under section 1705, with the limitation that funding to pay the credit subsidy costs of leading-edge biofuel projects eligible under this section would not exceed $500 million. Congress later authorized the President to transfer up to $2 billion of the nearly $6 billion to expand the "Cash for Clunkers" program. Pub. L. No. 111-47 (Aug. 7, 2009). The $2 billion was transferred to the Department of Transportation, leaving nearly $4 billion to cover credit subsidy costs of projects supported under section 1705. On August 10, 2010, Pub. L. No. 111-226 rescinded an additional $1.5 billion from the loan guarantee appropriation to pay for education-related jobs, Medicaid and other initiatives, further reducing funding available to $2.5 billion.

[10]Other requirements include that the workers employed on the project, including contractors or subcontractors, will be paid wages not less than prevailing on similar work in the locality in accordance with the Davis-Bacon Act. The act limited loan guarantees under section 1705 to the following categories of projects: (1) renewable energy systems, including incremental hydropower, that generate electricity or thermal energy, and facilities that manufacture related components; (2) electric power transmission systems, including upgrading and reconductoring projects; and (3) leading-edge biofuel projects that will use technologies performing at the pilot or demonstration scale that the Secretary determines are likely to become commercial technologies and will produce transportation fuels that substantially reduce life-cycle greenhouse gas emissions compared with other transportation fuels.

[11]New or significantly improved technology means a technology concerned with the production, consumption, or transportation of energy and that is not a commercial technology, and that has either: (1) only recently been developed, discovered, or learned; or (2) involves or constitutes one or more meaningful and important improvements in productivity or value, in comparison to commercial technologies in use in the United States at the time the term sheet is issued.

GAO-12-157 DOE Loan Guarantees

Because authority for the section 1705 loan guarantees expired on September 30, 2011, section 1703 is now the only remaining authority for the LGP. In April 2011, Congress appropriated $170 million to pay credit subsidy costs for section 1703 projects. Previously, these costs were to be paid exclusively by the applicants and were not federally funded. Congress also authorized DOE to extend eligibility under section 1703 to certain projects that had applied under section 1705 but did not receive a loan guarantee prior to the September 30, 2011, deadline.[12]

DOE has issued nine calls for applications to the LGP. Each of these nine "solicitations" has specified the energy technologies it targets and provided criteria for the LGP to determine project eligibility and the likelihood of applicants repaying their loans (see table 1).

Table 1: DOE Solicitations for Applications to the LGP

Name of solicitation	Date issued or updated	Description of eligible energy technology
Mixed 06	8/8/06	All technologies except for nuclear facilities and oil refineries.
Nuclear Front-End	6/30/08	Facilities for new uranium enrichment capacity and distribution.
Nuclear Power	6/30/08	Nuclear power facilities.
Energy efficiency and renewable energy or EERE 08	6/30/08	Innovative energy efficiency, renewable energy, and advanced energy transmission and distribution technologies.
Fossil	9/22/08	Coal-based power generation and industrial gasification facilities that incorporate carbon capture and sequestration or other beneficial uses of carbon and for advanced coal gasification facilities.
Energy efficiency and renewable energy or EERE 09	7/29/09	Innovating energy efficiency, renewable energy, and advanced energy transmission and distribution technologies.
Transmission	7/29/09	Electric power transmission infrastructure investment projects.

[12]Department of Defense and Full-Year Continuing Appropriations Act, 2011, Pub. L No. 112-10.

Name of solicitation	Date issued or updated	Description of eligible energy technology
Financial Institution Partnership Program (FIPP)	10/7/09	Renewable energy generation projects using commercial technology.
Manufacturing	8/10/10	Manufacture of renewable energy systems and components using commercial technology.

Source: DOE.

To help ensure that that these criteria were applied consistently and that each selected project provided a reasonable prospect of repayment, in March 2009, the LGP issued a credit policies and procedures manual for the program, outlining its policies and procedures for reviewing loan guarantee applications. As shown in figure 1, this review process is divided into three stages: intake, due diligence, and "conditional commitment to closing." We use the term "review process" to refer to the entire process.

Figure 1: Overview of LGP Review Process for Applications through the Intake, Due Diligence, and Conditional Commitment to Closing Stages

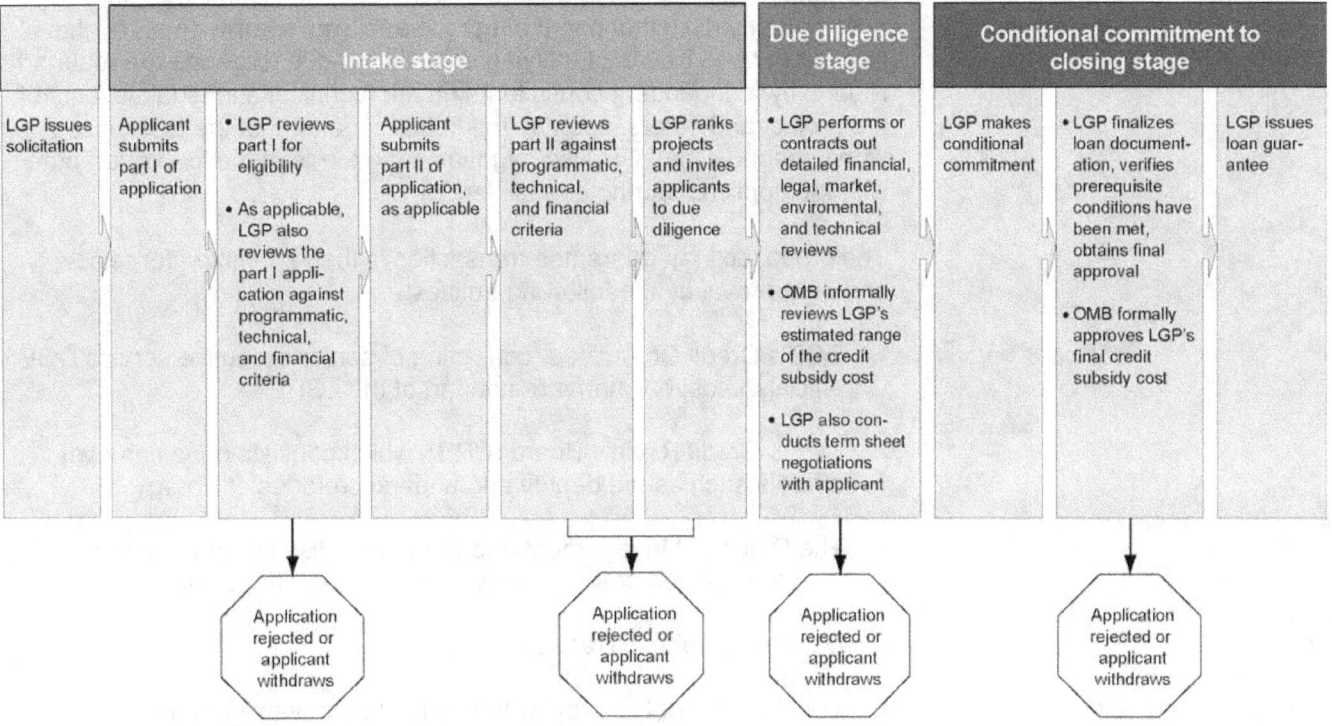

Source: GAO presentation of DOE data.

During the intake stage, the LGP assesses applications in a two-part process for most applicants. In part I, the LGP considers a project's eligibility based on the requirements in the solicitation and relevant laws and regulations. Nuclear solicitation applications are also evaluated against programmatic, technical, and financial criteria during the part I review. Based on the LGP's eligibility determination during part I review, qualifying applicants are invited to submit a part II application. Generally, LGP evaluates this application against programmatic, technical, and financial criteria to form a basis for ranking applications within each solicitation.[13] Based on these initial rankings, the LGP selects certain

---

[13]Under the FIPP solicitation, applicants must apply to a private "lead lender," which initially evaluates the proposed loan guarantee for credit approval and decides whether to apply to DOE for the loan guarantee.

GAO-12-157 DOE Loan Guarantees

applications for the due diligence stage. During due diligence, the LGP performs a detailed examination of the project's financial, technical, legal, and other qualifications to ensure that the LGP has identified and mitigated any risks that might affect the applicant's ability to repay the loan guarantee. Key to identifying risks during due diligence are required reports by independent consultants on the technical and legal aspects of the project and others, such as marketing reports, that the LGP uses when needed. The LGP also negotiates the terms of the loan guarantee with the applicant during due diligence.

The proposed loan guarantee transaction is then submitted for review and/or approval by the following entities:

- DOE's Credit Committee, consisting of senior executive service DOE officials, most of whom are not part of the LGP.

- DOE's Credit Review Board (CRB), which consists of senior-level officials such as the deputy and undersecretaries of Energy.

- The Office of Management and Budget (OMB), which reviews the LGP's estimated credit subsidy range for each transaction.

- Department of the Treasury.

- The Secretary of Energy, who has final approval authority.

Following the Secretary's approval, the LGP offers the applicant a "conditional commitment" for a loan guarantee. If the applicant signs and returns the conditional commitment offer with the required fee, the offer becomes a conditional commitment, contingent on the applicant meeting conditions prior to closing. During the conditional commitment to closing stage, LGP officials and outside counsel prepare the final financing documents and ensure that the applicant has met all conditions required for closing, and the LGP obtains formal approval of the final credit subsidy cost from OMB. Prior to closing, applications may be rejected by the LGP. Similarly, applicants can withdraw at any point during the review process. Once these steps have been completed, the LGP "closes" the loan guarantee and, subject to the terms and conditions of the loan guarantee agreement, begins to disburse funds to the project. For further detail on the review process, see appendix III.

DOE Has Made $15.1 Billion in Loan Guarantees but Does Not Maintain Consolidated Data on Status of Applications

For 460 applications to the LGP from its nine solicitations, DOE has made $15.1 billion in loan guarantees and conditionally committed to an additional $15 billion, representing $30 billion of the $34 billion in loan guarantees authorized for the LGP.[14] However, when we requested data from the LGP on the status of the applications to its nine solicitations, the LGP did not have consolidated data readily available but had to assemble them from various sources.

DOE Has Made $15.1 Billion in Loan Guarantees and Committed to Another $15 Billion

As of September 30, 2011, the LGP had received 460 applications and made (closed) $15.1 billion in loan guarantees in response to 30 applications (7 percent of all applications), all under section 1705. It had not closed any guarantees under section 1703. In addition, the LGP had conditionally committed another $15 billion for 10 more applications (2 percent of all applications)—4 under section 1705 and 6 under section 1703. The closed loan guarantees obligated $1.9 billion of the $2.5 billion in credit subsidy appropriations funded by the Recovery Act for section 1705, leaving $600 million of the funds unused before the program expired. For section 1703 credit subsidy costs, the $170 million that Congress appropriated in April 2011 to pay such costs is available, but it may not cover all such costs because the legislation makes the funds available only for renewable energy or efficient end-use energy technologies.[15] Applicants whose projects' credit subsidy costs are not covered by the appropriation must pay their own credit subsidy costs. To date, credit subsidy costs for loan guarantees that DOE has closed have, on average, been about 12.5 percent of the guaranteed loan amounts.

The median loan guarantee requested for all applications was $141 million. Applications for nuclear power projects requested significantly larger loan amounts—a median of $7 billion—and requested the largest

---

[14]The amount of authority does not include approximately $20 billion that expired when authority for a portion of the program expired on September 30, 2011.

[15]The legislation also made some section 1705 projects submitted to DOE by Feb. 24, 2011, eligible for these funds, but nuclear projects are not included among eligible projects.

total dollar amount by type of technology—$117 billion.[16] Applications for energy efficiency and renewable energy solicitations requested the second-largest dollar amount—$74 billion. Table 2 provides further details on the applications by solicitation and the resulting closed loan guarantees and conditional commitments. Appendix II provides further details on the individual committed and closed loan guarantees.

Table 2: Number of Applications, Median and Total Loan Guarantees Requested, Total Conditionally Committed Loan Guarantees, and Total Closed Loan Guarantees, by Solicitation, through September 30, 2011

Dollars in millions

Solicitation, issue date	Number of applications	Median loan guarantee requested	Total loan guarantee requested	Total conditionally committed loan guarantee	Total closed loan guarantee[a]
Mixed 06, 8/8/06	140	$60[b]	$31,018[b]	$72[e]	$1,203
Energy Efficiency and Renewable Energy 08, 6/30/08[c]	68	163	21,265	261[e]	3,381
Nuclear Front-End, 6/30/08	2	2,000	4,000	2,000[e]	0
Nuclear Power, 6/30/08	19	6,969	117,363	8,326[e]	0
Fossil, 9/22/08	8	2,072	17,145	0	0
Energy Efficiency and Renewable Energy 09, 7/29/09	168	150	52,915	2,105	5,601
Transmission, 7/29/09	12	660	11,586	0	343
Financial Institution Partnership Program, 10/7/09	37	146	11,057	2,274	4,516
Manufacturing, 8/10/10	6	98	1,022	0	0
Total	**460**	**$141[d]**	**$267,372**	**$15,038[e]**	**$15,044**

Source: GAO analysis of DOE data provided as of July 29, 2011, and updated for new commitments or closings, as of September 30, 2011.

Note: Totals may not add due to rounding.

[a]Fifteen of these guarantees went to projects that applied under section 1703 but were later deemed eligible for and received funding under section 1705.

[16]The minimum loan guarantee requested for all applications was $0, and the maximum loan guarantee requested was $12 billion, both for nuclear power projects. The $0 loan guarantee request was for one portion of a jointly sponsored nuclear power project. The joint sponsor of the nuclear power project requested approximately $8 billion in loan guarantees.

[b]The median and total loan guarantee amounts reflect the reported loan amounts for 134 of the 140 Mixed 06 applications because DOE said 6 applicants did not specify the amount of their loan guarantee request.

[c]This row includes four applications that LGP does not consider to be official submissions since the applicants did not pay the application fee. However, we included these applications in our analysis because the LGP included them in the application data they provided to us, and these applications demonstrate the level of interest in the solicitation.

[d]This amount is the median loan guarantee amount requested across all solicitations. The minimum loan guarantee requested for all applications was $0, and the maximum loan guarantee requested was $12 billion, both for nuclear power projects.

[e]Of the $15 billion in committed loan guarantees, applications under the section 1703 authority to these solicitations account for $10.4 billion or 71 percent. See appendix II for a list of these committed loan guarantees.

For all 460 LGP applications submitted, figure 2 shows the total loan guarantee amounts requested by type of energy technology.

Figure 2: Amount of Loan Guarantees Requested in 460 Applications by Energy Technology Category, as of July 29, 2011

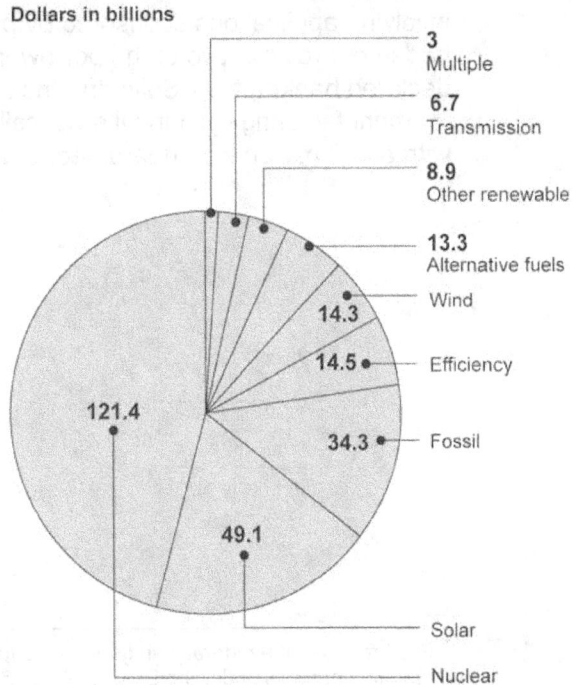

Dollars in billions

3 Multiple
6.7 Transmission
8.9 Other renewable
13.3 Alternative fuels
14.3 Wind
14.5 Efficiency
34.3 Fossil
49.1 Solar
121.4 Nuclear

Source: GAO analysis of DOE data describing the energy technology of each loan guarantee application, as of July 29, 2011

Note: For this analysis, we used simplified energy technology categories based on DOE's data. The figure omits one application for which the LGP did not report the type of energy technology employed by the proposed project or the amount requested for the project. It also omits requests that DOE listed as using "other" energy technology, which totaled about 0.01 percent of the amount requested.

Table 3 provides an overview, as of September 30, 2011, of the status of the 460 loan guarantee applications that the LGP received in response to its nine solicitations. Of the 460 applications, 66 were still in various stages of the approval process (intake and due diligence), 40 had received conditional commitment or were closed, and 354 had been withdrawn or rejected. DOE documents list a wide range of reasons for application withdrawals, including inability to submit application material in a timely manner, inability to secure feedstock, project faced many hurdles, applicant did not pursue project, and applicant switched to another program. Solicitations that primarily targeted efficiency and renewable energy received the most applications, while those targeting nuclear front-end technologies (for the beginning of the nuclear fuel cycle), manufacturing, and fossil fuels received the fewest. The rejection rate was highest for applications submitted for two of the earlier solicitations and much lower for DOE's FIPP,[17] a more recent solicitation involving applications sponsored by private financial institutions. Since we began our review, two of the borrowers with closed loan guarantees have declared bankruptcy—Solyndra, Inc., with a $535 million loan guarantee for manufacturing cylindrical solar cells, and Beacon Power Corporation, with a $43 million loan guarantee for an energy storage technology.

[17]FIPP refers to the federal loan guarantees for commercial technology renewable energy generation projects under the DOE LGP solicitation number DE-FOA-0000166, dated October 7, 2009. This solicitation is unique because it is the only one inviting private lenders to share due diligence activities for identifying and mitigating risk and finance a portion of total project costs.

Table 3: Number (and Percentage) of Applications in Each Review Stage, by Solicitation, as of September 30, 2011

Solicitation, issue date	Number of applications	Number (percentage) of applications by stage					
		Intake	Due diligence	Conditional commitment	Guarantees made (closed)	Withdrawn	Rejected
Mixed 06, 8/8/06	140	0(0)	3(2)	1(1)	4(3)	8(6)	124(89)
EERE 08, 6/30/08[a]	68	0(0)	7(10)	2(3)	8(12)	6(9)	45(66)
Nuclear Front End, 6/30/08	2	0(0)	1(50)	1(50)	0(0)	0(0)	0(0)
Nuclear Power, 6/30/08	19	5(26)	4(21)	3(16)	0(0)	7(37)	0(0)
Fossil, 9/22/08	8	0(0)	4(50)	0(0)	0(0)	3(38)	1(13)
EERE 09, 7/29/09	168	12(7)	21(13)	1(1)	10(6)	59(35)	65(39)
Transmission, 7/29/09	12	2(17)	0(0)	0(0)	1(8)	9(75)	0(0)
Financial Institution Partnership Program (FIPP), 10/7/09	37	0(0)	7(19)	2(5)	7(19)	18(49)	3(8)
Manufacturing, 8/10/10	6	0(0)	0(0)	0(0)	0(0)	3(50)	3(50)
Total[b]	460	19(4)	47(10)	10(2)[c]	30(7)[d]	113(25)	241(52)

Source: GAO analysis of DOE data provided as of July 29, 2011 and updated for new commitments or closings as of September 30, 2011.

[a]This row includes four applications that the LGP does not consider to be official submissions since the applicants did not pay the application fee. However, we included these applications in our analysis because the LGP included them in the application data they provided to us, and these applications demonstrate the level of interest in the solicitation.

[b]Percentage totals may not add to 100 due to rounding.

[c]Four of these conditional commitments are under section 1705, and six are under section 1703. Many of the section 1703 applications have been in process since 2008 or before. See appendix II, tables 7 and 8.

[d]All of these closed loan guarantees are under section 1705. See appendix II, table 9.

The elapsed time for LGP to process loan applications generally decreased over the course of the program, according to LGP data. LGP officials noted that the elapsed time between review stages includes the time the LGP waited for the applicants to prepare required documents for each stage. The process was longest for applications to the earlier solicitations, issued solely under section 1703, from start to closing.[18] The review process was shorter for applications under the four more recent solicitations, issued after the passage of section 1705. For example, the

---

[18]Some closed loan guarantees went to projects that applied under section 1703 but were later eligible for and received funding under section 1705.

first solicitation, known as Mixed 06, had the longest overall time frames from intake to closing—a median of 1,442 days—and the FIPP solicitation had the shortest time frames—a median of 422 days.[19] Applications to the FIPP solicitation had the shortest elapsed time because this program was carried out in conjunction with private lenders, who conducted their own reviews before submitting loan applications to the LGP.[20] Table 4 shows the median number of days elapsed during each review stage, by solicitation, as of September 30, 2011.

Table 4: Number of Applications and Median Number of Days Elapsed During Each Review Stage and Overall, by Solicitation

Solicitation, issue date	Number of applications	Intake stage (parts I & II)	Due diligence stage	Conditional commitment to closing stage	Overall: start of intake to closing date	Rejected applications: start of intake to rejection date
Number of applications completing this stage		114	43	30	30	241
Mixed 06, 8/8/06	140	722	430	284	1,442	280
EERE 08, 6/30/08[a]	68	90	338	177	696	168
Nuclear Front-End, 6/30/08	2	230	401	b	b	b
Nuclear Power, 6/30/08	19	219	294	b	b	b
Fossil, 9/22/08	8	199	b	b	b	201
EERE 09, 7/29/09	168	194	309	114	668	70
Transmission, 7/29/09	12	178	222	115	515	b
FIPP, 10/7/09	37	73	228	92	422	94
Manufacturing, 8/10/10	6	b	b	b	b	78
Median number of days for all applications		**184[c]**	**294[d]**	**127[e]**	**660[f]**	**277[g]**

Source: GAO analysis of DOE data.

Notes:

The number of days elapsed represents the median for the review period of those applications that proceeded to the next review stage. We believe the median is a better representation of the data for this table because it reduces the effect of some outliers that skew the data.

[19]The minimum number of days elapsed from intake to closing was 287 days, and the maximum number of days from intake to closing was 1,731 days.

[20]The LGP's lenders to date have been the U.S. Treasury's Federal Financing Bank and the private lenders under the FIPP solicitation who brought applicants to the LGP and who must risk at least 20 percent of the total loans for the applicants' project.

The calculations were for the status and elapsed days of the 460 applications as of September 30, 2011.

The elapsed time between review stages includes the time the LGP waited for the applicant to prepare required documents for each stage.

[a]This row includes four applications that the LGP does not consider to be official submissions since the applicants did not pay the application fee. However, we included these applications in our analysis because the LGP included them in the application data they provided to us, and these applications demonstrate the level of interest in the solicitation. Additionally, the average elapsed time for intake review of applications to the EERE 08 solicitation is lower because applications for certain types of projects were not required to follow a two-part application process.

[b]No applications completed this stage for this solicitation.

[c]The minimum number of days elapsed for all applications for intake was 33 and the maximum number of days elapsed was 740.

[d]The minimum number of days elapsed for all applications for due diligence was 50 and the maximum number of days elapsed was 930.

[e]The minimum number of days elapsed for all applications for conditional commitment to closing was 41 and the maximum number of days elapsed was 407.

[f]The minimum number of days elapsed for all applications from intake to closing was 287 and the maximum number of days elapsed was 1,731.

[g]The minimum number of days elapsed for all applications from intake to rejection was 9 and the maximum number of days elapsed was 1,046.

From September 4, 2009, to July 29, 2011—a period of nearly 2 years— the LGP closed $5.8 billion in loan guarantees for 13 applications under section 1705. In the last few months before the authority for section 1705 loan guarantees expired, the LGP accelerated its closings of section 1705 applications that had reached the conditional commitment stage. Thus, over the last 2 months before the authority for section 1705 expired, the LPG closed an additional $9.3 billion in loan guarantees for 17 applications under section 1705.[21] The program did not use about $600 million of the $2.5 billion that Congress appropriated to pay credit subsidy costs before the section 1705 authority expired, and these funds were no longer available for use by LGP.

_____

[21]This effort was preceded by DOE's announcement on May 10, 2011, that the LGP would focus on 18 applications that officials believed were most likely to meet all the requirements for closing and begin construction prior to the September 30, 2011, expiration date.

The LGP Does Not Maintain Consolidated Information on Application Status

When we requested data from the LGP on the identity of applicants, status, and key dates for review of all the applications to its nine solicitations, the LGP did not have consolidated information on application status readily available. Instead, it had to assemble these data from various sources.

To respond to our initial data request, LGP staff provided information from the following five sources:

- "Origination portfolio" spreadsheets, which contain information for applications that are in the due diligence stage of the review process. These spreadsheets contain identifying information, the solicitation applied under, commitment or closing status, type of technology, overall cost, proposed or closed loan amount, and expected or actual approval dates. Information in these spreadsheets is limited. For example, they do not contain dates that the applicant completed each stage and do not have information on applications that have been rejected or withdrawn.

- "Tear sheet" summaries for each application, which give current status and basic facts about the project and its technology, cost, finances, and strengths and weaknesses. Tear sheets are updated periodically, or as needed, but LGP officials could not easily consolidate them because they were kept in word processing software that does not have analysis or summarization capabilities.

- "Application trackers," which are spreadsheets that give basic descriptive information and status of applications for some solicitations. LGP staff said they were maintained for most, but not all, solicitations.

- "Project Tracking Information" documents showing graphic presentations of application status summaries, loan guarantee amounts requested, technology type, planned processing dates, and procurement schedules for technical reports. These documents were updated manually through December 20, 2010.

- "Credit subsidy forecasts," which are documents that track the actual or projected credit subsidy costs of the section 1705 projects in various stages of the review process and the cumulative utilization of credit subsidy funding.

LGP staff needed over 3 months to assemble the data and fully resolve all the errors and omissions we identified. LGP staff also made further changes to some of these data when we presented our analysis of the data to the LGP in October 2011.[22] According to LGP officials in 2010, the program had not maintained up-to-date and consolidated documents and data. An LGP official said at the time that LGP considered it more important to process loan guarantee applications than to update records. Because it took months to assemble the information required for our review, it is also clear that the LGP could not be conducting timely oversight of the program. Federal regulations require that records be kept to facilitate an effective and accurate audit and performance evaluation. These regulations—along with guidance from the Department of the Treasury and OMB—provide that maintaining adequate and proper records of agency activities is essential to oversight of the management of public resources.[23]

In addition, under federal internal control standards, federal agencies are to employ control activities, such as accurately and promptly recording transactions and events to maintain their relevance and value to management on controlling operations and making decisions.[24] Under these standards, managers are to compare actual program performance to planned or expected results and analyze significant differences. Managers cannot readily conduct such analysis of the LGP if the agency does not maintain consolidated information on applications to the program and their status. Moreover, the fact that it took the LGP 3 months to aggregate data on the status of applications for us suggests that its managers have not had readily accessible and up-to-date information and have not been doing such analysis on an ongoing basis. This is not consistent with one of the fundamental concepts of internal control, in which such control is not a single event but a series of actions and activities that occur throughout an entity's operations and on an ongoing

---

[22]Errors and omissions included missing or incorrect dates associated with an applicant's progression to the next stage of LGP review; incorrect status (e.g., application listed as both withdrawn and rejected); inconsistent entries related to the loan guarantee amount requested by the applicant; and no status given.

[23]10 C.F.R. § 609.10(f)(1); U.S. Department of the Treasury, *Managing Federal Receivables A Guide for Managing Loans and Administrative Debt,* Financial Management Service (Washington, D.C.: 2005); and OMB Circular A-130.

[24]GAO, *Standards for Internal Control in the Federal Government,* GAO/AIMD-00-21.3.1 (Washington, D.C.: November 1999).

basis. Thus, providing managers with access to aggregated, updated data could facilitate more efficient management of the LGP.

Furthermore, without consolidated data about applicants, LGP actions, and application status, LGP staff may not be able to identify weaknesses, if any, in the program's application review process and approval procedures. For example, consolidated data on application status would provide a comprehensive snapshot of which steps of the review process are taking longer than expected and may need to be addressed. If program data were consolidated in an electronic tracking system, program managers could quickly access information important to managing the LGP, such as the current amount of credit subsidy obligated, as well as whether the agency is consistently complying with certain procedural requirements under its policies and regulations that govern the program. In addition, the program cannot quickly respond to requests for information about the program as a whole from Congress or program auditors.

In March 2011, the LGP acknowledged the need for such a system. According to the March 2011 LGP summary of its proposed data management project, as the number of applications, volume of data and records, and number of employees increased, the existing method for storing and organizing program data and documents had become inadequate, and needed to be replaced. In October 2011, LGP officials stated that while the LGP has not maintained a consolidated application tracking database across all solicitations, the program has started to develop a more comprehensive business management system that includes a records management system called "iPortal" that also could be used to track the status of applications. Officials did not provide a timetable for using iPortal to track the status of applications but said that work is under way on it. However, until iPortal or some other system can track applications' status, the LGP staff cannot be assured that consolidated information on application status necessary to better manage the program will be available.

The LGP Did Not Always Adhere to Its Review Process, Which May Pose Risks and Result in Inconsistent Treatment

We identified 43 key steps in the LGP's guidance establishing its review process for assessing and approving loan guarantee applications. The LGP followed most of its established review process, but the LGP's actual process differed from this established process at least once on 11 of the 13 applications we reviewed, in part because the process was outdated. In some cases, LGP did not perform applicable review steps and in other cases we could not determine whether the LGP had completed review steps. Furthermore, we identified more than 80 instances of deficiencies in documentation of the LGP's reviews of the 13 applications, such as missing signatures or dates. It is too early to evaluate the impact of the specific differences we identified on achieving program goals, but we and the DOE Inspector General have reported that omitting or poorly documenting review steps may pose increased financial risk to the taxpayer and result in inconsistent treatment of applications.

The LGP Did Not Consistently Follow Its Established Review Process, in Part Because the Process Was Outdated

We identified 43 key steps in the LGP credit policies and procedures manual and its other guidance that establish the LGP's review process for assessing and approving loan guarantee applications. Not all 43 steps are necessary for every application, since the LGP's guidance lets officials tailor aspects of the review process on an ad hoc basis to reflect the specific needs of the solicitation. For example, under the EERE 08 solicitation, the LGP required two parts of intake review for applications involving large projects that integrate multiple types of technologies, but it required only one part for small projects. Furthermore, according to LGP officials, they have changed the review process over time to improve efficiency and transparency, so the number of relevant steps also depends on when the LGP started reviewing a given application. LGP guidance recognizes the need for such flexibility and maintains that program standards and internal control need to be applied transparently and uniformly to protect the financial interests of the government. For more information on the key steps we identified, see appendix III.

According to private lenders we contacted who finance energy projects, the LGP's established review process is generally as stringent as or more stringent than those lenders' own due diligence processes. For example, like the LGP, private lenders evaluate a project's proposed expenses and income in detail to determine whether it will generate sufficient funds to support its debt payments. In addition, private lenders and the LGP both rely on third-party expertise to evaluate the technical, legal, and marketing risks that might affect the payments. Lenders who were not participating in the LGP generally agreed that the LGP's process, if followed, should provide reasonable management of risk. Some lenders that sponsored applications under the FIPP solicitation said that the LGP's review process was more rigorous than their own. They said this level of rigor was not warranted for the FIPP solicitation because it covered commercial technology, which is inherently less risky than the innovative technologies covered by other solicitations. Some private lenders we spoke with also noted that financing an innovative energy project involves a certain amount of risk that cannot be eliminated, and one lender said that a failure rate of 2 or 3 percent is common, even for the most experienced loan officers.

However, we found that the LGP did not always follow the review process in its guidance. The LGP completed most of the applicable review steps for the 6 applications that we reviewed in full, but its actual process differed from the established process at least once on 5 of the 6 applications we reviewed. We also conducted a more limited examination of 7 additional applications, in which we examined the steps where the actual process differed from the established process for the first 6 applications. We again found that the LGP's actual process differed from its established process at least once on 6 of the 7 applications. Table 4 summarizes review steps for which we either identified differences or could not determine whether the LGP completed a particular review step across all 13 applications. The 13 applications we reviewed represent all of the applications that had reached conditional commitment or closing, as of December 31, 2010, excluding 3 applications that had applied under the earliest solicitation, since the LGP's review process was substantially different for these 3 applications.[25]

---

[25]The three excluded applications were from Solyndra, Beacon Power, and Sage Electrochromics, LLC. One of the 13 applications we reviewed was for a project with multiple sponsors. In this instance, we only reviewed the application with the largest loan guarantee amount request.

Table 5: LGP's Adherence to Its Review Process for 13 Applications with Closed or Conditionally Committed Loan Guarantees, by Review Stage and Step

Review stage	Review step description	Number of applications examined for review step	Not applicable	Applicable but not performed	Could not determine if step was performed	Completed
Intake	Part I technical review	6	2	0	1	3
	Solicitation-specific ranking process for EERE 08 applicants	13	5	0	8	0
	Obtain CRB approval prior to due diligence	13	3	6	0	4
Due diligence	Review of applicant's management (e.g., background check, credit check, Internal Revenue Service check)	6	0	2	1	3
	Obtain final independent engineering report prior to conditional commitment	13	0	6	0	7
	Obtain final independent marketing report prior to conditional commitment	13	3	1	1	8
	Complete OMB review of the LGP credit subsidy cost estimate	13	0	3	7	3
Conditional commitment to closing	Collect a full fee from an applicant at conditional commitment	13	0	1	0	12
Total			**13**	**19**	**18**	**40**

Source: GAO analysis of LGP documentation supporting its application reviews.

Note: These differences represent our review of LGP documents for all 43 key review steps for six applications, and a targeted review of 9 steps for seven applications.

For the 13 applications we examined, we found 19 differences between the actual reviews the LGP conducted and the applicable review process steps established in LGP guidance. In most of these instances, according to LGP officials, the LGP did not perform an applicable review step because it had made changes intended to improve the process but had not updated the program's credit policies and procedures manual or other guidance governing the review process.

The following describes the 19 differences we identified, along with the LGP's explanations:

- In six cases, the LGP did not obtain CRB approval prior to due diligence, contrary to the March 2009 version of its credit policies and procedures manual. This version states that CRB approval is an important internal check to ensure only the most promising projects proceed to due diligence. LGP officials explained that this step was not necessary for these applications because the CRB had verbally delegated to the LGP its authority to approve applications before these projects proceeded to due diligence. However, LGP documents indicate that CRB delegated approval authority after these projects had proceeded to due diligence.[26] According to an LGP official, the delegation of authority was not retroactive.

- In seven cases, the LGP did not obtain final due diligence reports from independent consultants prior to conditional commitment, as required by its credit policies and procedures manual. Through their reporting, these independent third parties provide key input to the LGP's loan underwriting and credit subsidy analyses in technical, legal, and other areas such as marketing, as necessary. LGP officials said that it was a preferable practice to proceed to conditional commitment with drafts of these reports and obtain a final report just prior to closing. They said this practice helps the LGP reduce financial risk, since it allows the LGP to base its decision to close the loan guarantee on final reports rather than reports completed 1 to several months earlier. An LGP official explained that this part of the review process had evolved to meet the program's needs, but that these changes were not yet reflected in the manual. However, the LGP does not appear to have implemented this change consistently. Specifically, over the course of several months in 2009 and 2010, the LGP alternated between the old and the new process concerning final due diligence reports from independent consultants. In commenting on a draft of this report, LGP officials said that in all cases they received final independent consultant reports before the closing of the loan guarantees. Because the LGP's policies and procedures manual at the time required final reports at the conditional commitment stage, we reviewed the reports available at conditional commitment and did not review whether LGP received final reports before closing.

---

[26]The documents LGP provided for this step indicated that the CRB decision to delegate its authority occurred on June 25, 2009. The projects in question proceeded to due diligence in May 2009.

- In three cases, the LGP conditionally committed to a loan guarantee before OMB had completed its informal review of the LGP's credit subsidy cost estimate. According to the credit policies and procedures manual, OMB should be notified each time the LGP estimates the credit subsidy cost range, and informal discussions between OMB and LGP should ensue about the LGP estimate. This cost is to be paid by the borrower for all section 1703 projects to date and by the federal government for section 1705 projects. LGP officials explained that, in two of these cases, the LGP had provided OMB with their credit subsidy estimates, but that OMB had not completed its review because there were unresolved issues with the LGP estimates. LGP officials did not provide an explanation for the third case. Contrary to the manual, LGP officials said that OMB's informal review of the credit subsidy estimates for these applications was not a necessary prerequisite to conditional commitment because the actual credit subsidy cost is calculated just prior to closing and is formally approved by OMB. Furthermore, under section 1705, the government rather than the borrower, was to pay credit subsidy costs. Accordingly, the LGP used these credit subsidy estimates for internal planning purposes rather than for calculating a fee to the applicant. In contrast, the LGP completed OMB's informal review prior to conditionally committing to at least three of the other loan guarantees we reviewed—including one section 1705 project—and thus the LGP did not perform this step consistently across all projects. In its October 2011 update of its credit policies and procedures manual, the LGP retained the requirement that OMB review the LGP's credit subsidy cost estimate prior to conditional commitment. Further, the updated guidance added that formal discussions with OMB may be required each time OMB reviews LGP's credit subsidy cost estimate and should result with their approval.

  In two cases, the LGP did not complete its required background check for project participants. The documents provided indicate that LGP did not determine whether the applicants had any delinquent federal debt prior to conditional commitment. In one of these cases, LGP officials said that the delinquent federal debt check was completed after conditional commitment. In the other case, the documents indicate that the sponsor did not provide a statement on delinquent debt, and LGP officials confirmed that LGP did not perform the delinquent debt check prior to conditional commitment.

- In one case, the LGP did not collect the full fee from an applicant at conditional commitment as required by the EERE 08 solicitation. According to a LGP official, the LGP changed its policy to require 20 percent of this fee at conditional commitment instead of the full fee specified in the solicitation, in response to applicant feedback. This official said the policy change was documented in the EERE 09 solicitation, which was published on July 29, 2009. However, this particular application moved to conditional commitment on July 10, 2009, prior to the formal policy change.

As outlined in these cases, the LGP departed from its established procedures because, in part, the procedures had not been updated to reflect all current review practices. The version of the manual in use at the time of GAO's review was dated March 5, 2009, even though the manual states that it was meant to be updated at least on an annual basis and more frequently if needed. The LGP issued its first update of its credit policies and procedures manual on October 6, 2011,[27] even though the 2009 manual states that it was meant to be updated at least annually and more frequently if needed. We reviewed the revised manual and found that the revisions addressed many of the differences that we identified between the LGP's established and actual review processes. The revised manual also states that LGP analyses should be properly documented and stored in the new LGP electronic records management system. However, the revised guidance applies to loan guarantee applications processed after October 6, 2011, but not to the 13 applications we reviewed or to any of the 30 loan guarantees the LGP has closed to date.

The LGP Did Not Always Fully Document Review Steps

In addition to the differences between the actual and established review processes, in another 18 cases, we could not determine whether the LGP had performed a given review step. In some of these cases, the documentation did not demonstrate that the LGP had applied the required criteria. In other cases, the documentation the LGP provided did not show that the step had been performed. The following discusses these cases:

- In one case, we could not determine whether LGP guidance calls for separate part I and part II technical reviews for a nuclear front-end application or allows for a combined part I and part II technical review. The LGP performed a combined part I and part II technical review.

---

[27]U.S. Department of Energy, *Credit Policies and Procedures Manual for Implementing Title XVII of the Energy Policy Act of 2005, Revised*, Loan Programs Office (Washington, D.C.: Oct. 6, 2011).

- In eight cases, we could not determine the extent to which the LGP applied the required criteria for ranking applications to the EERE 08 solicitation. The LGP's guidance for this solicitation requires this step to identify "early mover" projects for expedited due diligence. The LGP expedited four such applications but the documentation neither demonstrated how the LGP used the required criteria to select applications to expedite nor why other applications were not selected.

- In one case, we could not determine whether the LGP completed its required background check for project participants. The documents provided indicated there were unresolved questions involving one participant's involvement in a $17 billion bankruptcy and another's pending civil suit.

- In one case, we could not determine whether the LGP had received a draft or final marketing report prior to conditional commitment in accordance with its guidance. The LGP provided a copy of the report prepared before closing but did not provide reports prepared before conditional commitment.

- In seven cases, LGP either did not provide documents supporting OMB's completion of its informal review of the LGP's estimated credit subsidy range before conditional commitment, or the documentation the LGP provided was inconclusive.

We also found 82 additional documentation deficiencies in the 13 applications we reviewed. For example, in some cases, there were no dates or authors on the LGP documents. The documentation deficiencies make it difficult to determine, for example, whether steps occurred in the correct order or were executed by the appropriate official. The review stage with the fewest documentation deficiencies was conditional commitment to closing, when 1 of the 82 deficiencies occurred. Table 6 shows the instances of deficient documentation that we identified.

Table 6: Documentation Deficiencies Identified During 13 Application Reviews

Review phase	Missing author	Missing title or other identification	Missing final version or a signature	Missing date	Missing data or analysis	Inconsistent with other project documents
Intake	15	6	2	17	8	1
Due diligence	12	0	6	6	5	3
Conditional commitment to closing	0	0	0	0	0	1
Total	27	6	8	23	13	5

Source: GAO analysis of LGP documentation supporting its application reviews.

Note: These deficiencies represent our review of LGP documents for all 43 review steps for six applications and a targeted review of 9 steps for seven applications.

During our review, the LGP did not have a central paper or electronic file containing all the documents supporting the key review steps we identified as being part of the review process. Instead, these documents were stored separately by various LGP staff and contractors in paper files and various electronic storage media. As a result, the documents were neither readily available for us to examine, nor could the LGP provide us with complete documentation in a timely manner. For example, we requested documents supporting the LGP's review for six applicants in January 2011. For one of the applications, we did not receive any of the requested documents supporting the LGP's intake application reviews until April 2011. Furthermore, for some of the review steps, we did not receive documents responsive to our request until November 2011 and, as we discussed earlier, in 18 cases we did not receive sufficient documentation to determine whether the LGP performed a given review step. Federal regulations and guidance from Treasury and OMB provide that maintaining adequate and proper records of agency activities is essential to accountability in the management of public resources and the protection of the legal and financial rights of the government and the public.[28] Furthermore, under the federal standards for internal control, agencies are to clearly document internal control, and the documentation is to be readily available for examination in paper or electronic form.

---

[28]36 C.F.R. § 1222.22; U.S. Department of the Treasury, *Managing Federal Receivables A Guide for Managing Loans and Administrative Debt,* Financial Management Service (Washington, D.C.: 2005) and OMB Circular A-130.

Moreover, the standards state that all documentation and records should be properly managed and maintained.[29]

As stated above, the LGP recognized the need for a recordkeeping system to properly manage and maintain documentation supporting project reviews. In March 2011, the LGP adopted a new records management system called "iPortal" to electronically store documents related to each loan application and issued guidance for using this system. As of November 1, 2011, LGP officials told us that the system was populated with data or records relevant to conditionally committed and closed loan guarantees and that they plan to fully populate it with documentation of the remaining applications in a few months. The LGP was able to provide us with some additional documents from its new system in response to an early draft of this report, but the LGP did not provide additional documentation sufficient to respond to all of the issues we identified. Accordingly, other oversight efforts may encounter similar problems with documentation despite the new system.

Differences Between the Actual and Established Processes and Incomplete Documentation May Pose Risks

It is too early in the loan guarantees' terms to assess whether skipping or poorly documenting review steps will result in problems with the guarantees or the program. However, we and the DOE Inspector General have reported that omitting or poorly documenting review steps may lead to a risk of default or other serious consequences. Skipping or poorly documenting steps of the process during intake can lead to several problems. First, it reduces the LGP's assurance that it has treated applications consistently and equitably. This, in turn, raises the risk that the LGP will not select the projects most likely to meet its goals, which include deploying new energy technologies and ensuring a reasonable prospect of repayment. In July 2010, we reported that the inconsistent treatment of applicants to the LGP could also undermine public confidence in the legitimacy of the LGP's decisions. Furthermore, DOE's Inspector General reported in March 2011 that incomplete records may impede the LGP's ability to ensure consistency in the administration of

---

[29]GAO/AIMD-00-21.3 states in part that internal control and all transactions and other significant events need to be clearly documented, and the documentation should be readily available for examination. OMB Circular A-130, *Management of Federal Information Resources* requires agencies to ensure that records management adequately document agency activities and ensure access to the records regardless of form or medium.

the program, make informed decisions, and provide information to Congress, OMB, and other oversight bodies.[30] The Inspector General also stated that, in the event of legal action related to an application, poor documentation of the LGP's decisions may hurt its ability to prove that it applied its procedures consistently and treated applicants equitably. Moreover, incomplete records may leave DOE open to criticism that it exposed taxpayers to unacceptable financial risks.

Differences between the actual and established review processes that occur during or after due diligence may also lead to serious consequences. These stages of the review process were established to help the LGP identify and mitigate risks. Omitting or poorly documenting its decisions during these stages may affect the LGP's ability to fully assess and communicate the technical, financial, and other risks associated with projects. This could lead the program to issue guarantees to projects that pose an unacceptable risk of default. Complete and thorough documentation of decisions would further enable DOE to monitor the loan guarantees as projects are developed and implemented. Furthermore, without consistent documentation, the LGP may not be able to fully measure its performance and identify any weaknesses in its implementation of internal procedures.

Conclusions

Through the over $30 billion in loan guarantees and loan guarantee commitments for new and commercial energy technologies that DOE has made to date, the agency has set in motion a substantial federal effort to promote energy technology innovation and create jobs. DOE has also demonstrated its ability to make section 1705 of the program functional by closing on 30 loan guarantees. It has also improved the speed at which it was able to move section 1705 applications through its review process. To date, DOE has committed to six loan guarantees under section 1703 of the program, but it has not closed any section 1703 loan guarantees or otherwise demonstrated that the program is fully functional. Many of the section 1703 applications have been in process since 2008 or before. As DOE continues to implement section 1703 of the LGP, it is even more important that it fully implement a consolidated system for overseeing the application review process and that LGP adhere to its review process and

---

[30]U.S. Department of Energy, Office of Inspector General, *Audit Report: The Department of Energy's Loan Guarantee Program for Clean Energy Technologies,* DOE/IG-0849 (Washington, D.C.: Mar. 3, 2011).

GAO-12-157 DOE Loan Guarantees

document decisions made under updated policies and procedures. It is noteworthy that the process LGP developed for performing due diligence on loan guarantee applications may equal or exceed those used by private lenders to assess and mitigate project risks. However, DOE does not have a consolidated system for documenting and tracking its progress in reviewing applications fully implemented at this time. As a result, DOE may not readily access the information needed to manage the program effectively and to help ensure accountability for federal resources. Proper recordkeeping and documentation of program actions is essential to effective program management. The absence of such documentation may have prevented LGP managers, DOE, and Congress from having access to the timely and accurate information on applications necessary to manage the program, mitigate risk, report progress, and measure program performance. DOE began to implement a new records management system in 2011, and LGP staff stated that the new system will enable them to determine the status of loan guarantee applications and to document review decisions. However, the LGP has neither fully populated the system with data or records on all applications it has received nor its decisions on them. Nor has DOE committed to a timetable to complete the implementation of the new records management system. Until the system has been fully implemented, it is unclear whether the system will enable the LGP to both track applications and adequately document its review decisions.

In addition, DOE did not always follow its own process for reviewing applications and documenting its analysis and decisions, potentially increasing the taxpayer's exposure to financial risk from an applicant's default. DOE has not promptly updated its credit policies and procedures manual to reflect its changes in program practices, which has resulted in inconsistent application of those policies and procedures. It also has not completely documented its analysis and decisions made during reviews, which may undermine applicants' and the public's confidence in the legitimacy of its decisions. Furthermore, the absence of adequate documentation may make it difficult for DOE to defend its decisions on loan guarantees as sound and fair if it is questioned about the justification for and equity of those decisions. DOE has recently updated its credit policies and procedures manual, which, if followed and kept up to date, should help the agency address this issue.

Recommendations for Executive Action

To better ensure that LGP managers, DOE, and Congress have access to timely and accurate information on applications and reviews necessary to manage the program effectively and to mitigate risks, we recommend that the Secretary of Energy direct the Executive Director of the Loan Programs Office to take the following three actions:

- Commit to a timetable to fully implement a consolidated system that enables the tracking of the status of applications and that measures overall program performance.

- Ensure that the new records management system contains documents supporting past decisions, as well as those in the future.

- Regularly update the LGP's credit policies and procedures manual to reflect current program practices to help ensure consistent treatment for applications to the program.

Agency Comments and Our Evaluation

We provided a copy of our draft report to DOE for review and comment. In written comments signed by the Acting Executive Director of the Loan Programs Office, it was unclear whether DOE generally agreed with our recommendations. The Acting Executive Director stated subsequently to the comment letter that DOE disagreed with the first recommendation and agreed with second and third recommendations. In its written comments, DOE also provided technical and editorial comments, which were incorporated as appropriate. DOE's comments and our responses to specific points can be found in appendix IV of this report.

Concerning our first recommendation that LGP commit to a timetable to fully implement a consolidated system that enables the tracking of the status of applications and that measures overall program performance, in its written comments, DOE states that the LGP believes that it is important that our report distinguish between application tracking and records management. We believe we have adequately distinguished the need for application tracking and management of documentation. These are addressed in separate sections of our report and in separate recommendations. DOE also states that LGP has placed a high priority on records management and is currently implementing a consolidated state-of-the-art records management system. In the statement subsequent to DOE's written comments, the Acting Executive Director stated the office did not agree to a hard timetable for implementing our first recommendation. As stated in the report draft, under federal internal control standards, agencies are to employ control activities, such as accurately and promptly recording transactions and events to maintain their relevance and value to management on controlling operations and making decisions. Because LGP had to manually assemble the application status information we needed for this review, and because this process took over 3 months to accomplish, we continue to believe DOE should develop a consolidated system that enables the tracking of the status of applications and that measures overall program performance. This type of information will help LGP better manage the program and respond to requests for information from Congress, auditors, or other interested parties.

Concerning our second recommendation that LGP ensure that its new records management system contains documents supporting past decisions as well as those in the future, subsequent to DOE's written comments, the Acting Executive Director stated that DOE agreed.

Concerning our third recommendation that LGP regularly update the credit policies and procedures manual to reflect current program practices, subsequent to DOE's written comments, the Acting Executive Director stated that DOE agreed.

We are sending copies of this report to the appropriate congressional committees, the Secretary of Energy, and other interested parties. In addition, this report also is available at no charge on the GAO website at http://www.gao.gov.

If you or your staff members have any questions about this report, please contact me at (202) 512-3841 or ruscof@gao.gov. Contact points for our Offices of Congressional Relations and Public Affairs may be found on the last page of this report. GAO staff that made major contributions to this report are listed in appendix V.

Frank Rusco
Director, Natural Resources and Environment

Appendix I: Objectives, Scope, and Methodology

This appendix details the methods we used to examine the Department of Energy's (DOE) Loan Guarantee Program (LGP). We have reported four times and testified three times on this program, including two previous reports in response to the mandate in the 2007 Revised Continuing Appropriations Resolution to review DOE's execution of the LGP and to report our findings to the House and Senate Committees on Appropriations. (See Related GAO Products.) Because of questions regarding inconsistent treatment of applications raised by the most recent report in this mandated series,[1] this report, also in response to the mandate, assesses (1) the status of the applications to the LGP's nine solicitations and (2) the extent to which the LGP has adhered to its process for reviewing applications for loans that the LGP has committed to or closed.

To gather information on the program, we met with the LGP's management and staff from each of the program's divisions involved with the LGP's review of loan guarantee applications from intake to closing. In general, we reviewed the laws, regulations, policies and procedures governing the program and pertinent agency documents, such as solicitations announcing loan guarantee opportunities. We reviewed prior GAO and DOE Inspector General reports performed under or related to our mandate to audit the LGP. In addition, we gathered agency data and documents on the loan guarantee applications in process, those that had received a DOE commitment, and those that had been closed.

To determine the status of the applications to all nine of the solicitations for our first objective, we explored the LGP's available sources to see what data the program had compiled on the applications received and their current status in the review process. Because the LGP did not have comprehensive or complete application status data, we tailored a data request to collect data on the status of all 460 applications to the program. In consultation with agency officials, we prepared a data collection form requesting basic information on the identity, authority, amount requested, status, key milestone dates, and type of energy technology for all of the applications to date. These data were to provide a current snapshot of the program by solicitation and allow analysis of various characteristics. To ease the data collection burden, we populated the spreadsheets for each solicitation with the limited data from available

---

[1]GAO-10-627.

sources. LGP staff or contractors familiar with each solicitation completed the spreadsheets, and these spreadsheets were reviewed by managers before they were forwarded to GAO. We assessed the reliability of the data the LGP provided by reviewing these data, comparing them to other sources, and following up repeatedly with the agency to clarify questions and inconsistencies, and obtain missing data. This process enabled us to develop up-to-date program-wide information on the status of applications. This process resulted in data that were complete enough to describe the status of the program. Once we collected these data, we found them to be sufficiently reliable for our purposes. The LGP updated its March 2011 applicant status data as of July 29, 2011, and we obtained additional data on the conditional commitments and closings made by the September 30, 2011, expiration of the section 1705 authority for loan guarantees with a credit subsidy. To maintain consistency between the application status data initially provided by the LGP and later data updates, we use the terms application and project interchangeably, although in some cases multiple applications were submitted for a single project.

To assess the LGP's execution of its review process for our second objective, we first analyzed the law, regulations, policies, procedures, and published solicitations for the program and interviewed agency staff to identify the criteria and the key review process steps for loan guarantees, as well as the documents that supported the process. We provided a list of the key review steps we identified to LGP officials, and incorporated their feedback as appropriate. Based on the key review steps and supporting documentation identified by LGP staff, we developed a data collection instrument to analyze LGP documents and determine whether the LGP followed its review process for the applications reviewed. Since the LGP's review process varied across solicitations, we tailored the data collection instrument to meet the needs of the individual solicitations. We then selected a nonprobability sample of 6 applications from the 13 that had received conditional commitments from DOE or had progressed to closing by December 31, 2010, and had not applied under the Mixed 2006 solicitation, since the LGP's review process was substantially different for this solicitation and not directly comparable to later solicitations.[2] We requested documentation for these 6 applications

---

[2]The three excluded Mixed 2006 applications were from Solyndra, Beacon Power, and Sage Electrochromics, LLC. One of the 13 applications we reviewed was for a project with multiple sponsors. In this instance, we only reviewed the application with the largest loan guarantee amount request.

representing a range of solicitations and project types. We selected our
initial sample to represent each of the five solicitations where applications
had reached conditional commitment and different LGP investment
officers to reduce the burden on LGP staff. We requested the documents
supporting the LGP's review process from intake to closing and examined
them to determine whether the applicable review steps were carried out.
While we examined whether the applicable review steps were carried out,
we did not examine the content of the documents and the quality of work
supporting them. Where the documents were not clear about completion
of the process, showed potential differences from the review process, or
raised questions, we followed up with program officials to obtain an
explanation and, as applicable, documentation supporting the
explanation. On key questions where we identified differences from the
review process for the initial sample of 6, we conducted a targeted review
of documents for the 7 remaining applications that had reached
conditional commitment or closed prior to December 31, 2010, excluding
Mixed 2006 applicants. The six loan guarantee application files reviewed
in full and the seven files reviewed in part were a nongeneralizable
sample of applications.

To identify the initial universe of private lenders with experience financing
energy projects, we reviewed the list of financial institutions that had
submitted applications to the LGP under the Financial Institution
Partnership Program (FIPP) solicitation. We used these firms as a
starting point because of their knowledge about DOE's program and
processes. To identify financial institutions involved in energy sector
project finance outside of FIPP, we searched or contacted industry
associations, industry conferences, and other industry groups in the same
energy sectors that LGP solicitations to date have targeted. We
interviewed seven private lenders identified through this process using a
set of standard questions and the outline of the DOE's review process to
gain insights on its comparability to the review process for underwriting
loans in the private sector.

We conducted this performance audit from September 2010 to February
2012 in accordance with generally accepted government auditing
standards. Those standards require that we plan and perform the audit to
obtain sufficient, appropriate evidence to provide a reasonable basis for
our findings and conclusions based on our audit objectives. We believe
that the evidence obtained provides a reasonable basis for our findings
and conclusions based on our audit objectives.

Appendix II: Tables of Loan Guarantees Conditionally Committed or Closed

The following tables provide basic details on the loan guarantee applications that received a conditional commitment by September 30, 2011, or had proceeded to closing by that date. Table 7 lists applications under section 1703 with conditional commitments. Table 8 lists section 1705-eligible applications with conditional commitments that did not reach closing by the expiration of the section 1705 authority on September 30, 2011. Table 9 lists the section 1705 applications with conditional commitments that reached closing by the expiration of the section of the 1705 authority on September 30, 2011.

Table 7: Section 1703 Applications Reaching Conditional Commitment as of September 30, 2011, by Solicitation

Dollars in millions

Solicitation	Sponsor	Name	Technology	Date conditional commitment offered	Guarantee amount
Mixed, 8/8/06	SAGE Electrochromics, LLC	SAGE Electrochromics	Energy Efficiency	3/5/2010	$72
EERE 08, 6/30/08	ADA-ES, Inc.	Red River	Energy Efficiency	12/8/2009	245
Nuclear Front-End, 6/30/08	AREVA NC, Inc.	Eagle Rock Enrichment Facility	Nuclear Front-End	5/20/2010	2,000
Nuclear Power, 6/30/08	Georgia Power Company	Vogtle 3&4	Nuclear Generation	2/16/2010	3,460
Nuclear Power, 6/30/08	MEAG	Vogtle 3&4	Nuclear Generation	2/16/2010	1,809
Nuclear Power, 6/30/08	Oglethorpe Power Corp.	Vogtle 3&4	Nuclear Generation	2/16/2010	3,057
Total					**$10,643**

Source: GAO analysis of DOE data.

Table 8: Section 1705-Eligible Applications Reaching Conditional Commitment as of September 30, 2011, by Solicitation

Dollars in millions

Solicitation	Sponsor	Name	Technology	Date conditional commitment offered	Guarantee amount
EERE 08, 6/30/08	Nordic Windpower, Ltd.	Nordic Project	Wind Manufacturing	7/2/2009	$16
EERE 09, 7/29/09	Solar Millennium, LLC	Blythe Solar Power Project Plant	Solar Generation	4/18/2011	2,105
FIPP, 10/7/09	First Solar	Topaz (CA)	Solar Generation	6/30/2011	1,930
FIPP, 10/7/09	Multiple	SolarStrong (USA)	Solar Generation	9/8/2011	344
Total					**$4,395**

Source: GAO analysis of DOE data.

Table 9: Section 1705-Eligible Applications Reaching Closing as of September 30, 2011, By Solicitation

Dollars in millions

Solicitation	Sponsor	Name	Technology	Date conditional commitment offered	Date closed	Guarantee amount
Mixed, 8/8/06	Beacon Power Corp.	Beacon Power	Transmission	7/2/2009	8/6/2010	$43
Mixed, 8/8/06	BrightSource Energy, Inc.	Ivanpah 1	Solar Generation	2/22/2010	4/5/2011	520
Mixed, 8/8/06	POET, LLC	Project LIBERTY	Biomass	7/7/2011	9/23/2011	105
Mixed, 8/8/06	Solyndra, Inc.	Solyndra Fab 2, LLC	Solar Manufacturing	3/20/2009	9/4/2009	535
EERE 08, 6/30/08	Abengoa Solar, Inc.	Solana Project	Solar Generation	7/2/2010	12/20/2010	1,446
EERE 08, 6/30/08	Abound Solar, Inc.	Abound Solar Manufacturing, LLC	Solar Manufacturing	7/2/2010	12/9/2010	400
EERE 08, 6/30/08	AES Energy Storage, LLC	Project Dyno	Transmission	7/30/2010	12/22/2010	17
EERE 08, 6/30/08	BrightSouce Energy, Inc.	Ivanpah 2	Solar Generation	2/22/2010	4/5/2011	551
EERE 08, 6/30/08	BrightSouce Energy, Inc.	Ivanpah 3	Solar Generation	2/22/2010	4/5/2011	556
EERE 08, 6/30/08	First Wind Energy, LLC	Kahuku Wind Power	Wind Generation	2/18/2010	7/26/2010	117
EERE 08, 6/30/08	SoloPower, Inc.	SoloPower Manufacturing Facility	Solar Manufacturing	2/17/2011	8/19/2011	197
EERE 08, 6/30/08	U.S. Geothermal, Inc.	Neal Hot Springs	Geothermal	6/9/2010	2/23/2011	97
EERE 09, 7/29/09	1366 Technologies, Inc.	Project Eagle	Solar Maufacturing	6/17/2011	9/8/2011	150
EERE 09, 7/29/09	Abengoa Bioenergy U.S. Holding	Abengoa Bioenergy Biomass of Kansas	Biomass	8/19/2011	9/29/2011	132
EERE 09, 7/29/09	Abengoa Solar, Inc.	Mojave Solar Project	Solar Generation	6/14/2011	9/23/2011	1,202
EERE 09, 7/29/09	Cogentrix Solar Services, LLC	Alamosa Solar Generating Project	Solar Generation	5/10/2011	9/9/2011	91
EERE 09, 7/29/09	Nextlight Renewable Energy, LLC	Antelope Valley Solar Ranch 1	Solar Generation	6/30/2011	9/30/2011	646
EERE 09, 7/29/09	Nextlight Renewable Energy, LLC	Agua Caliente	Solar Generation	1/20/2011	8/5/2011	967
EERE 09, 7/29/09	Sempra Generation	Mesquite Solar Energy	Solar Generation	6/15/2011	9/28/2011	337
EERE 09, 7/29/09	Solar Reserve, LLC	Tonopah Project	Solar Generation	5/19/2011	9/28/2011	737
EERE 09, 7/29/09	Sunpower Corp.	California Valley Solar Ranch	Solar Generation	4/12/2011	9/30/2011	1,237

Dollars in millions

Solicitation	Sponsor	Name	Technology	Date conditional commitment offered	Date closed	Guarantee amount
EERE 09, 7/29/09	Yale University	Record Hill Wind	Wind Generation	3/3/2011	8/15/2011	102
Transmission, 7/29/09	LS Power Associates, LP	Southwest Intertie Project (SWIP) - South	Transmission	10/19/2010	2/11/2011	343
FIPP, 10/7/09	Caithness Energy, LLC	Shepherds Flat (OR)	Wind Generation	10/8/2010	12/16/2010	1,051
FIPP, 10/7/09	First Solar	Desert Sun (CA)	Solar Generation	6/30/2011	9/30/2011	1,169
FIPP, 10/7/09	Nevada Geothermal Power Company	Blue Mountain (NV)	Geothermal	6/15/2010	9/3/2010	79
FIPP, 10/7/09	NextEra	Genesis Solar (CA)	Solar Generation	6/14/2011	8/26/2011	682
FIPP, 10/7/09	Noble Environmental Power, LLC	Noble Granite (NH)	Wind Generation	6/21/2011	9/23/2011	135
FIPP, 10/7/09	Ormat Nevada, Inc.	Ormat (NV)	Geothermal	6/9/2011	9/23/2011	280
FIPP, 10/7/09	Prosun Solar Development Company, LLC	Project Amp (USA)	Solar Generation	6/22/2011	9/30/2011	1,120
Total						$15,044

Source: GAO analysis of DOE data.

Table 10 provides basic details about key review tasks in LGP's process for reviewing and approving loan guarantee applications, as identified from our review of relevant laws, regulations, LGP guidance, published solicitations and interviews with LGP officials. These tasks formed the basis for our examination of LGP files to determine if LGP followed its review process for each of the 13 applications that had received conditional commitments from DOE or had progressed to closing by December 31, 2010, and had not applied under the Mixed 2006 solicitation.[1] Accordingly, the tasks listed below reflect LGP's review process for the applications we reviewed and do not reflect LGP's review process for applicants to the Mixed 2006 solicitation, which was substantially different and not directly comparable to later solicitations. Additionally, since we found minor variations in LGP's review process across the solicitations, we have noted below which tasks are only applicable under certain solicitations. If no exceptions are listed, then the particular task is applicable across all the relevant solicitations.

Table 10: Key Review and Approval Tasks for Loan Guarantee Applications, by Review Stage

Review stage and task	Description
Intake	
1. Collect part I application fee.	The first of three fees that LGP collects during the review process. LGP is required by its authorizing legislation to charge and collect sufficient fees to cover the program's administrative costs.
2. Perform part I completeness check.	LGP reviews applications using a solicitation-specific checklist to document that the application package is complete.
3. Perform innovation review (*EERE 08 applicants*).	LGP reviews applications to determine if the proposed project uses an innovative energy technology, as required by the program's authorizing legislation. For later solicitations, this review was incorporated into the LGP's technical review.
4. Perform part I technical review (*2008 Nuclear Power and Nuclear Front-End*) or commercial review (*FIPP*).	LGP analyzes the project's eligibility and responsiveness to statutory and program requirements, such as the project's • technical relevance against DOE requirements, • technical approach and work plan, and • environmental and technological benefits.

---

[1]The three excluded Mixed 2006 applications were from Solyndra, Beacon Power, and Sage Electrochromics, LLC. One of the 13 applications we reviewed was for a project with multiple sponsors. In this instance, we only reviewed the application with the largest loan guarantee amount request.

Review stage and task	Description
5. Perform part I financial review (*2008 Nuclear Power and Nuclear Front-End*).	LGP analyzes • creditworthiness elements such as sponsor/management capabilities, financial/business plans, and market factors; and • programmatic elements such as (a) construction and start-up factors and (b) legal, regulatory, and permitting factors.
6. Perform emissions review or lifecycle analysis (*EERE 08 and EERE 09 applicants*).	Loan guarantee applications under the EERE 08 and EERE 09 solicitations must pass an emissions analysis to meet the authorizing law's greenhouse gas emissions goals.
7. Perform review for solicitation-specific eligibility requirements.[a]	Depending on the solicitation, loan guarantee applications must meet certain solicitation-specific eligibility requirements, related to • certain project types, • certain technology categories, and • construction commencement requirements for section 1705 projects.
8.a. Rank projects to identify "Early Movers" (*EERE 08 only*).	LGP identifies the projects that present the fewest obstacles in moving forward to begin the technical and financial review process first. The ranking factors are related to • level of environmental review required under the National Environmental Policy Act of 1970, • financial structure, • readiness to proceed, and • offtake agreements if applicable (an agreement to buy all or a substantial part of the output of an energy project).
8.b. Rank Projects and Identify Project Strengths and Weaknesses as part of the part I review (*2008 Nuclear Power and Nuclear Front-End*).	The 2008 Nuclear Power and Front-End solicitations call for an early ranking of projects. The ranking factors are related to • the prospect of repayment, • strength of the project and sponsor, and • regulatory status.
9. Notify applicants of intent to proceed/invite part II submissions (*part II submissions exclude certain EERE 08 projects*).	For solicitations with a one-part intake process, applicants are notified of LGP's intent to proceed with its review. For solicitations with a two-part intake process, applicants are notified they have qualified under part I and are invited to submit application materials for part II.
10. Collect part II application fee.[b]	The second of three fees that LGP collects during the review process. LGP is required by the authorizing legislation to charge and collect sufficient fees to cover the program's administrative costs.
11. Perform part II completeness check.	LGP reviews applications using a solicitation-specific checklist to document that the part II application package is complete.
12. Perform part II technical review (*excludes FIPP*).	LGP analyzes • the project's technical relevance against DOE requirements, • track record and experience of applicant, • project work plan, and • environmental benefits of project.

Appendix III: Key Tasks in the LGP's Review
and Approval Process for Loan Guarantee
Applications

Review stage and task	Description
13. Perform part II financial review (*excludes FIPP*).	LGP analyze • creditworthiness elements such as sponsor/management capabilities, financial/business plans, and market factors; and • programmatic elements such as (a) construction and start-up factors and (b) legal, regulatory, and permitting factors.
14. Perform an environmental critique and synopsis.	LGP may prepare a publicly available environmental critique and synopsis to document the consideration given to environmental factors and record that the relevant environmental consequence of each alternative has been considered in its evaluation and selection process.
15. Application screening/ranking sessions for finalization of merit review scores for selections to due diligence.	To focus limited loan guarantee funds on the best applicants, LGP evaluates and competitively ranks all applications within each solicitation's cohort. This ranking is the basis for LGP's decision to invite applicants to due diligence.
16. DOE's Credit Review Board (CRB) approves projects recommended for due diligence by LGP (*only projects proceeding to due diligence prior to 6/25/09*).	DOE's CRB reviews LGP's recommendations of projects for due diligence and provides approval. The CRB delegated this authority to LGP on June 25, 2009, and this task was phased out for applications proceeding to due diligence following this decision.
17. Notify applicant of LGP's decision to proceed into due diligence (*excludes FIPP*).	After clearing requirements of parts I and II, the applicants are notified that they will proceed into due diligence.
Due diligence	
18. Evaluate financing plan and assess financial viability.	To evaluate the project in detail, LGP will • thoroughly review the uses and sources of funds; • analyze adequacy, leverage, timing of funding; • review terms/rights of funding source; • assess the adequacy of proposed contingency/reserve funding; • determine compliance with program requirements from the law, final regulations, and the solicitation; • assess the project's financial viability, with an emphasis on the applicant's ability to repay the guaranteed portion of loan; and • evaluate assumptions underlying projected revenues/expenses/likelihood technical performance will be achieved.
19. Perform a review of applicant's management.	LGP performs certain checks (e.g., background check, credit check, IRS check) to evaluate the key players for the loan guarantee applicant.
20. Evaluate project risks and identify risk mitigants.	To evaluate the project's risks and potential mitigants, LGP will • identify, assess, and estimate the impact of risks associated with the project; • determine the types and magnitude of the risks associated with the project; • determine the proper risk allocation among the parties; and • determine the extent to which risks have been mitigated.
21. Perform a financial model analysis and stress-test.	To evaluate the project's financial model, LGP will • verify the applicant's calculations for its financial model, and • quantify the impacts of risks by stress-testing the applicant's and LGP's financial models for changes in assumptions.

Appendix III: Key Tasks in the LGP's Review
and Approval Process for Loan Guarantee
Applications

Review stage and task	Description
22. Assess strengths and weaknesses of project participants.	LGP will examine the sponsor's investment to date and financial/managerial capability to implement the project as proposed, including • the project sponsor's track record in project development and the technology used in the application, • the project sponsor's financial strength and resources, • the strategic value of the project to the sponsor, and • the experience of the project's management team.
23. Assess whether an environmental assessment, environmental impact statement, or categorical exclusion applies. (*For FIPP projects, this assessment step occurs during intake.*)	As required by the National Environmental Policy Act of 1970 (NEPA), LGP reviews the project and determines which environmental review process is necessary.
24. Prepare Environmental Assessment, Environmental Impact Statement or Categorical Exclusion.	Based on LGP's analysis under task 23, LGP prepares the appropriate documents, which include a description of any significant findings under other applicable environmental laws.
25. Identify significant findings under other applicable environmental laws.	
26. Receive independent engineering/technical consultant report.	To determine the technical efficacy of the project, LGP or an independent engineering firm, will thoroughly review the applicant's independent engineering report, including consideration of factors such as environmental impact and infrastructure requirements. This review also provides input for the risks and mitigants section of the credit paper.
27. Receive independent legal analysis.	To review the project's legal structure, LGP or an external firm will • analyze draft legal agreements among project participants, • analyze intellectual property rights of participants in the project to use the proposed technology, and • provide input for the risks and mitigants section of the credit paper.
28. Receive independent marketing consultant report (as applicable).	As necessary, LGP will consult with external marketing advisors to assess the project's market and off-take risk as part of the underwriting and credit analysis process. This assessment should be supported by data, examples, and/or research that substantiate the score assigned for each attribute.
29. Negotiate term sheet.	Based on its due diligence analysis and input from any external advisors, LGP prepares a term sheet and negotiates its provisions with the applicant.
30. Calculate expected recovery rate.	LGP calculates the percentage of value the agency can expect to recover in the event of default.
31. Prepare a credit approval package.	LGP assembles key documents describing the proposed loan guarantee agreement and project for internal review. These include • the credit paper providing an overview of the project and its attributes, • available third-party input, • draft term sheet, • internal risk rating matrix, • recovery rate notching matrix, • compliance checklist, and • presentation summarizing the transaction for internal and external review.

**Appendix III: Key Tasks in the LGP's Review
and Approval Process for Loan Guarantee
Applications**

Review stage and task	Description
32. Credit committee reviews and approves the credit approval package.	LGP management internal review and approval step.
33. Office of Management and Budget (OMB) reviews LGP's credit subsidy estimate.	OMB reviews LGP's calculation of the estimated credit subsidy cost range for the project and provides informal approval. The credit subsidy cost is based on a formula designed to determine the net present value of the estimated cost to the federal government of guaranteeing the loan.
34. LGP consults with U.S. Treasury regarding the commitment of Federal Financing Bank funds.	The Department of the Treasury reviews the transaction.
35. DOE's CRB approves projects recommended by LGP for conditional commitment.	DOE leadership review and approval step.
Conditional commitment to closing	
36. DOE offers applicant conditional commitment for a loan guarantee and applicant accepts.	DOE conditionally commits to issuing a loan guarantee agreement dependent upon whether the conditions precedent laid out in the term sheet are met. Upon accepting the offer, the applicant pays all or a portion of the second fee, depending on the solicitation.
37. LGP prepares and negotiates definitive financing documentation	LGP and external counsel prepare and negotiate the final financing terms and loan guarantee agreement.
38. LGP receives final credit rating from a rating agency via the applicant.	The applicant obtains and provides final credit rating to LGP.
39. LGP legal team circulates an action memo to all relevant parties for concurrence and the Secretary's signature.	Internal review and approval step that includes a crosswalk between the key terms at the time of conditional commitment and the final closing terms, including any material adverse differences.
40. OMB formally approves the final credit subsidy cost.	OMB review and key decision step.
41. Outside counsel confirms that all conditions precedent to the loan guarantee agreement have been satisfied.	LGP asks outside counsel to verify that the applicant has met all of the terms agreed to at conditional commitment as preconditions for LGP's approval of the final loan guarantee agreement.
42. DOE and applicant execute loan agreement, and DOE issues guarantee.	The final loan guarantee documents are executed at closing and the loan is considered closed once the agreements have been executed.
43. First funds disbursement.	At the time of or shortly after the loan guarantee's closing, the Federal Financing Bank, or other lender, disburses the first payment of funds to the loan guarantee recipient.

Sources: GAO analysis of DOE guidance, published solicitations, and relevant regulations.

[a]According to LGP officials, this step is a component of the innovation and other eligibility reviews rather than a separate step. However, we included it as a separate step in our list of key review tasks since it was an important aspect of the process.

[b]As applicable, for solicitations where LGP established a two part application process for some or all applicants (*excludes stand-alone or manufacturing projects that applied under EERE 08*).

Appendix IV: Comments from the Department of Energy

Note: GAO comments supplementing those in the report text appear at the end of this appendix.

Department of Energy
Washington, DC 20585

FEB 2 3 2012

Mr. Frank Rusco
Director, Natural Resources and Environment
U.S. Government Accountability Office
441 G Street NW
Washington, D.C. 20548

Dear Mr. Rusco:

Thank you for the opportunity to comment on the Government Accountability Office's (GAO) draft report on the Department of Energy's (DOE or Department) Loan Guarantee Program (LGP), *Further Actions Are Needed to Improve Tracking and Review of Applications*. A draft statement of facts was provided to the Department for review on October 20, 2011, and a draft report was sent on January 19, 2012.

As the GAO's report makes clear, **commercial lenders interviewed by GAO have stated that LGP's underwriting and due diligence standards are as rigorous as, or more rigorous than, those in the private sector**. Specifically, GAO reports that:

➤ "According to private lenders we contacted who finance energy projects, the LGP's established review process is generally as stringent as or more stringent than those lenders' own due diligence processes."

➤ "Some lenders that sponsored applications under the FIPP [Financial Institution Partnership Program] solicitation said that the LGP's review process was more rigorous than their own."

➤ "Some private lenders we spoke with also noted that financing an innovative energy project involves a certain amount of risk that cannot be eliminated."

➤ "It is noteworthy that the process DOE developed for performing due diligence on loan guarantee applications equals or exceeds those used by private lenders to assess and mitigate project risks."

As the GAO report also noted, as of September 30, 2011, the LGP had made $16.2 billion in loan guarantees to 28 projects under Section 1705 of the Energy Policy Act of 2005. To put this in context, in the approximately two and one-half years since the Section 1705 program was authorized by Congress, **the Department managed to build and continuously improve an organization that has succeeded in making an unprecedented level of clean energy investments while maintaining standards that are as high or higher than major financial institutions in the United States**.

The LGP's portfolio includes a broad range of clean energy technologies under Title XVII, including two biomass projects, three geothermal power projects, 12 solar power generation projects, four solar manufacturing projects, three transmission/storage projects and four wind power generation projects.

The LGP has been recognized as an industry leader in the clean energy financing sector. In the recently published Bloomberg New Energy Finance Clean Energy and Energy Smart Technology League Tables, six of the "Asset Finance – Top 10 Deals" were LGP transactions, and LGP's loan guarantee support resulted in the Federal Financing Bank being ranked #1 in the

Printed with soy ink on recycled paper

"Asset Finance – Lead Arrangers" category. The #1 ranking reflects more than $10 billion in deal credit across 13 transactions.

While the GAO focused on recordkeeping within the loan program, the report should not be read as a comprehensive evaluation of the LGP. The GAO report acknowledged: "We did not evaluate the quality of the LGP's analyses supporting the completion of these [review] steps." As a result, the GAO's findings do not purport to assess the credit risks from the substantive quality of the LGP's underwriting of any transactions. DOE hopes that the GAO report makes clear to readers that the scope of GAO's review did not include an analysis of the merits and creditworthiness of any DOE loan guarantees. As an independent review by outside experts of the overall health of the loan program's portfolio recently concluded, the LGP's portfolio holds significantly less risk than that anticipated by Congress in funding the programs.

With respect to the GAO's findings on the LGP's recordkeeping, we note the following:

See comment 1.

➢ Most, if not all, of GAO's findings relate to procedures that the LGP had in place in 2009 and early 2010, rather than those in place during 2011 or 2012. The GAO acknowledged that its review only covered six applications (and it collected more limited information for seven projects) that had received conditional commitments or had closed by December 31, 2010, and five of those applications had previously been the subject of a GAO report from July 2010.

➢ The GAO did not review any of the 23 projects that received conditional commitments in 2011, nor does it account for any of the organizational, procedural, transactional, and system improvements the LGP has implemented during this period. The LGP continuously updates its processes, practices, and procedures to adapt to applicable market conditions and prudent industry standards.

See comment 2.

➢ Currently the LGP has a robust records management platform, and is in the process of deploying a consolidated state-of-the-art business management system. In addition, the LGP has designed, tested, and deployed a state-of-the art electronic portfolio management system.

See comment 3.

Enclosed please find the Department's response to GAO's recommendations and separate technical and factual comments on specific items in the draft report. While some of GAO's observations may have been valid in 2009 and early 2010, the LGP has since instituted many processes and systems not mentioned in the report that have addressed these concerns. It is therefore inappropriate to suggest that LGP oversight has in any way been ineffective without first considering the extent and value of these established and on-going process and system improvements.

The LGP remains committed to promoting the objectives of the Title XVII program and will continue to accelerate the commercial use of innovative technologies, contribute to economic growth, and promote projects that yield long term environmental benefits, at the same time maintaining program objectivity and protecting the interests of the American taxpayer.

Sincerely,

David G. Frantz
Acting Executive Director
Loan Programs Office

Enclosures

See comment 4.

U.S. Department of Energy
**GAO -12-157 – "Further Actions Are Needed to
Improve Tracking and Review of Applications"**

Response to the GAO Recommendations

GAO Recommendation: Commit to a timetable to fully implement a consolidated system that
enables the tracking of the status of applications and that measures overall program performance.

DOE Response: The LGP believes that it is important that the GAO report distinguish between
"project tracking" and "records management." LGP has placed a high priority on records
management and is currently implementing a consolidated state-of-the-art records management
system. This system should be distinguished from the GAO's concept of a consolidated "project
tracking" database across all LGP solicitations.

Each LGP solicitation is designed to provide unique application and project evaluation criteria.
The manufacturing or generation projects proposed under the various LGP solicitations cover a
wide range of nuclear energy, fossil fuels, renewable energy, and transmission technologies. The
Department utilizes a broad array of resources and expertise – scientific, engineering, financial,
environmental and legal – to analyze these highly differentiated projects and technologies. To
track projects, the Loan Guarantee Origination Division (Origination) intake team maintains
separate spreadsheets for each solicitation containing core project information and the status of
each application under consideration. Origination meets weekly to provide updates and discuss
developments on due diligence activities, which are then recorded in various DOE internal
reports. While the GAO report suggests that the LGP create a comprehensive "project tracking"
database across all solicitations, such a consolidated tracker is impractical for the highly varied
and specialized processes of the LGP.

To achieve its objectives, the LGP is organizing the voluminous records for each project in its
records management system to distinguish the evaluation bases employed for various
technologies and is employing a continuous improvement management approach in its robust
records management and comprehensive project tracking to ensure that LGP staff can readily
access the historical and current information they need on a day-to-day basis and over time.

In addition to continuously refining and enhancing its existing records management platform, the
LGP is in the process of deploying a consolidated state-of-the-art business management system,
and has designed, tested, and deployed a state-of-the art electronic portfolio management system.

GAO Recommendation: Ensure that the new records management system contains documents
supporting past decisions as well as those in the future.

DOE Response: The LGP has designed, developed, and deployed a portfolio management
system which will interface with the records management platform and maintain on-going
reports on all conditionally committed and closed projects. This integration will ensure that
historical records are organized and maintained appropriately and on-going project status reports
are retained and updated.

<u>GAO Recommendation</u>: Regularly update the LGP's credit policies and procedures manual to reflect current program practices to help ensure consistent treatment for applications to the program.

<u>DOE Response</u>: The LGP last updated its credit policies and procedures manual on October 6, 2011, and appreciates that GAO noted in its report that the updated manual addressed many of the differences GAO identified between the LGP's established and actual review processes. The LGP is committed to further updating its credit policies and procedures manual as appropriate.

The following are GAO's comments on the Department of Energy's letter dated February 23, 2012.

GAO Comments

1. We disagree with DOE's assertion that our findings relate only to procedures that LGP had in place in 2009 and early 2010. We compared LGP's actual process to its established process for each of the applications that reached closing or conditional commitment by December 31, 2010. As we note in the report, LGP did not revise its policies and procedures manual until October 2011, so the same established procedures were in place for all of the applications that closed by September 30, 2011. We did not review any of the applications that were committed or closed during 2011 in depth, in part because it took through November 2011 for LGP to respond to our repeated requests for available documentation for the applications closed or committed to through 2010. Our 2010 report on LGP (GAO-10-627) and this report had information on five of the same applications. We examined DOE's review process for these applications in much more depth for this report than in the previous one. We did take into account changes in LGP procedures, systems, and other improvements as part of our review, as noted by the references to LGP's new records management system and its updated policies and procedures manual. We also took into account changes in LGP policies and procedures that affected the 13 files that we reviewed, when LGP was able to document that these changes had occurred.

2. As noted in the report, these systems were not fully implemented at the time we were gathering data for our review and this is still the case, according to DOE's written comments, dated February 23, 2012.

3. As stated above, we disagree with LGP's statement that our findings relate only to procedures that LGP had in place in 2009 and early 2010. As we note in the report, LGP did not revise its policies and procedures manual until October 2011, so the same established procedures were in place for all of the applications that closed by September 30, 2011. The report describes LGP's efforts to update its documentation management and tracking systems and notes that none of these were fully implemented at the time of our review.

4. DOE disagrees with the recommendation to implement an application tracking system. However, as noted in our report and DOE's comments, LGP is in the process of implementing a consolidated

state of the art business management system that DOE believes may address this need. As we stated in the draft report, under federal internal control standards, federal agencies are to employ control activities, such as accurately and promptly recording transactions and events to maintain their relevance and value to management on controlling operations and making decisions. Because LGP had to manually assemble the application status information we needed for this review, and because this process took the program over three months to accomplish, we continue to believe DOE should develop a consolidated system that enables the tracking of the status of applications and that measures overall program performance. This type of information will help LGP better manage the program and respond to requests for information from Congress, auditors, or other interested parties.

Appendix V: GAO Contact and Staff Acknowledgments

GAO Contact	Frank Rusco (202) 512-3841 or ruscof@gao.gov
Staff Acknowledgments	In addition to the individual named above, Karla Springer, Assistant Director; Marcia Carlsen; Cindy Gilbert; Cathy Hurley; Emily Owens; John Scott; Ben Shouse; Carol Shulman; Barbara Timmerman; and Lisa Van Arsdale made key contributions to this report.

Related GAO Products

Recovery Act: Status of Department of Energy's Obligations and Spending. GAO-11-483T. Washington, D.C.: March 17, 2011.

Department Of Energy: Further Actions Are Needed to Improve DOE's Ability to Evaluate and Implement the Loan Guarantee Program. GAO-10-627. July 12, 2010.

Recovery Act: Factors Affecting the Department of Energy's Program Implementation. GAO-10-497T. March 4, 2010.

American Recovery and Reinvestment Act: GAO's Role in Helping to Ensure Accountability and Transparency for Science Funding. GAO-09-515T. March 19, 2009.

Department Of Energy: New Loan Guarantee Program Should Complete Activities Necessary For Effective and Accountable Program Management. GAO-08-750. July 7, 2008.

Department Of Energy: Observations On Actions To Implement The New Loan Guarantee Program For Innovative Technologies. GAO-07-798T. September 24, 2007.

The Department of Energy: Key Steps Needed to Help Ensure the Success of the New Loan Guarantee Program for Innovative Technologies by Better Managing Its Financial Risk. GAO-07-339R. February 28, 2007.

www.ingramcontent.com/pod-product-compliance
Lightning Source LLC
Chambersburg PA
CBHW081225170526
45165CB00009B/2955